Schirmer's Library of Musical Classics

Vol. 219

CHARLES DANCLA

OP. 74

ÉCOLE DU MÉCANISME
(SCHOOL OF MECHANISM)

FIFTY
DAILY EXERCISES

FOR THE

VIOLIN

EDITED

BY

GEORGE LEHMANN

ISBN 978-0-7935-5459-1

G. SCHIRMER, Inc.

DISTRIBUTED BY

HAL•LEONARD®
CORPORATION
7777 W. BLUEMOUND RD. P.O. BOX 13819 MILWAUKEE, WI 53213

School of Mechanism.
Fifty Daily Exercises.

CH. DANCLA. Op. 74.

The Exercises have been written expressly for the work of the left hand — to develop digital independence, uniformity and agility.

Moderato.

The fingers must fall from a sufficient height with force, elasticity and uniformity.

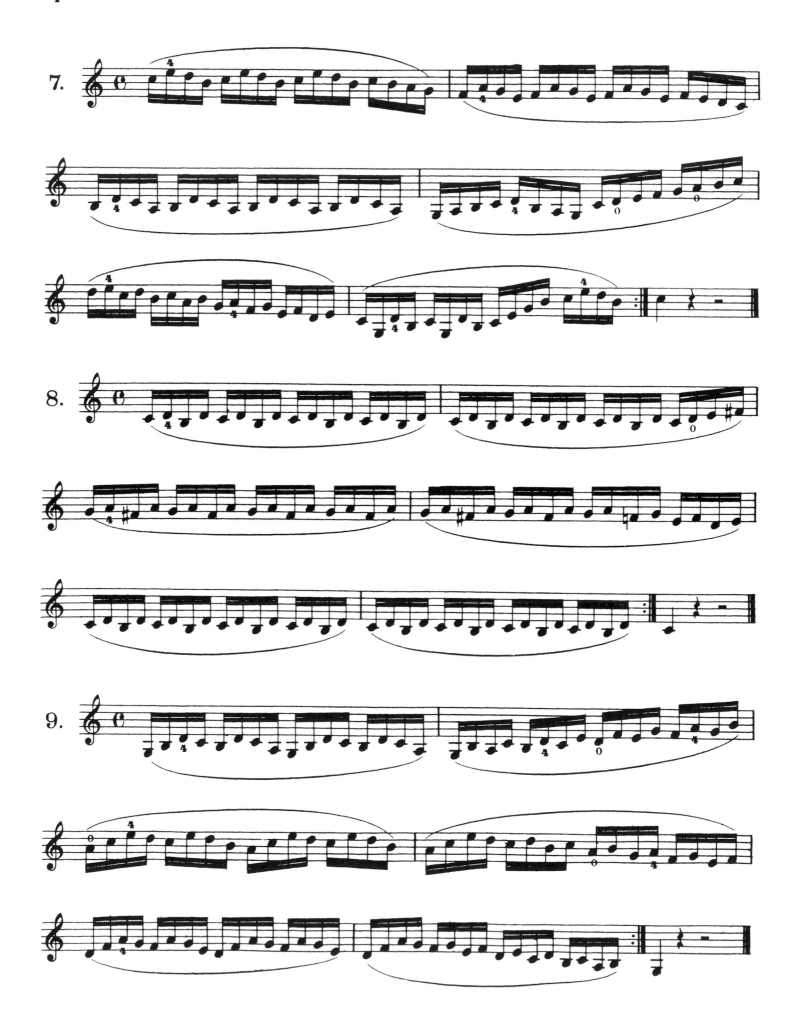

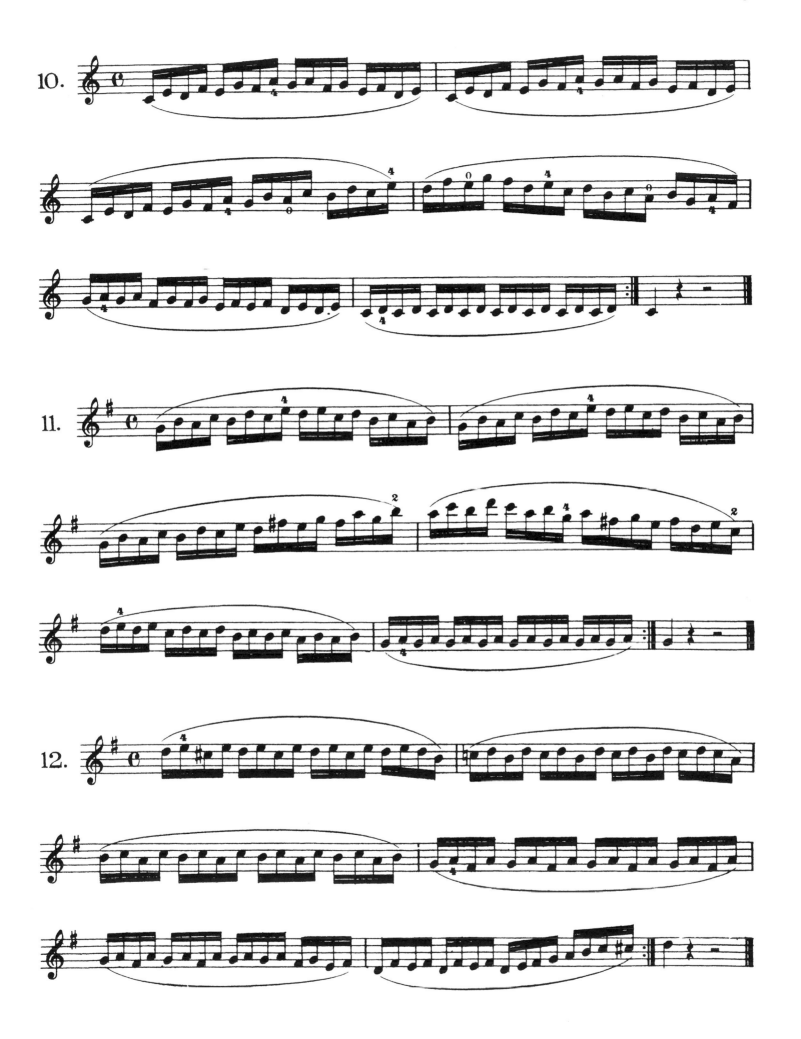

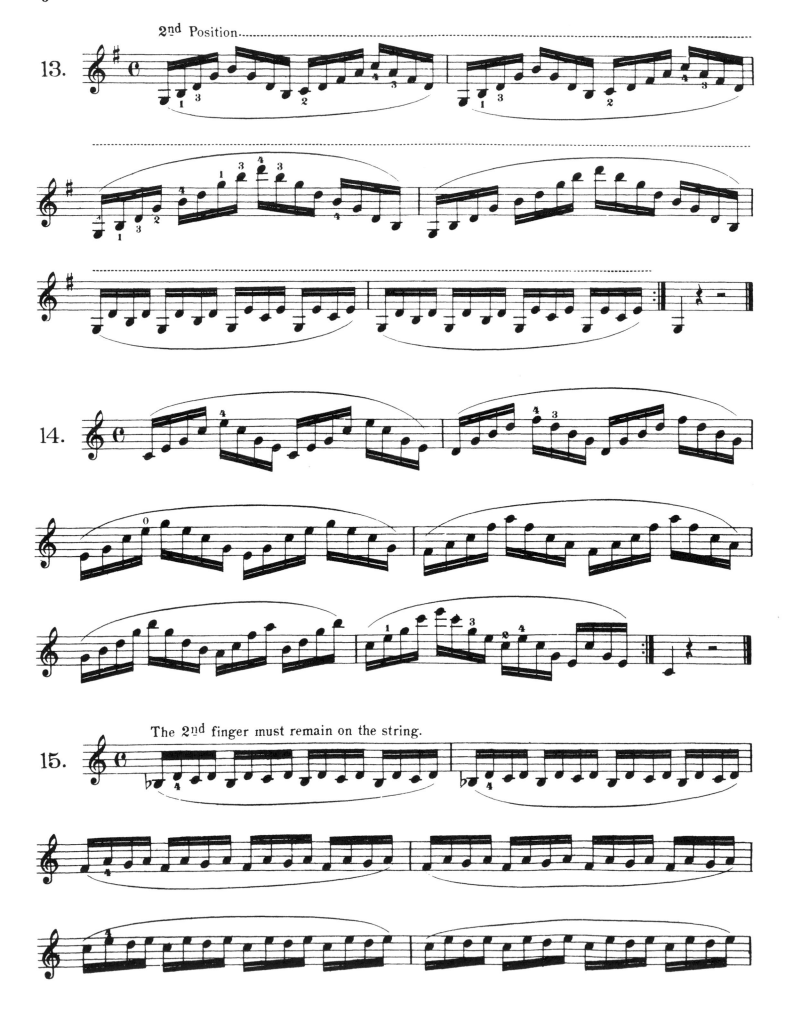

the 1st finger must remain on the string.

the second finger must remain on the string.

50.

restez..,

restez.